The twins go to visit Gr

Flick brings a pram. Fred brings his frog.

Gran is on the steps.

Hello, Gran.

Gran has a black cat.

Gran gets the twins a snack.

Flick spills her drink on the cloth. Gran is cross.

Fred drops his sandwich in the pram. Gran is cross.

But Spot the cat is glad.

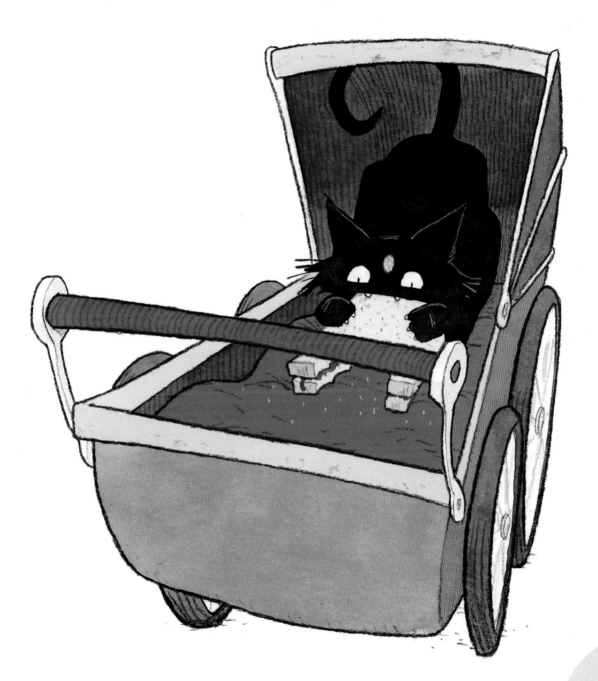

The frog jumps in the jam.
Fred grabs him.

Smash!
Gran is cross.

The frog jumps and jumps.
Spot runs and runs.

The frog jumps on the clock.
Gran is cross.

Stop!

At the end of the day the twins go home.

Gran is glad. The twins are glad.

But Spot is sad.